COLOSSIANS

by
Neva Evenhouse

revised by
Sylvia Boomsma

CRC Publications
Grand Rapids, Michigan

Unless otherwise noted, Scripture quotations in this publication are from the HOLY BIBLE, NEW INTERNATIONAL VERSION, © 1973, 1978, 1984, International Bible Society. Used by permission of Zondervan Bible Publishers.

Cover photo by Don Farall @ PhotoDisc

Discover Your Bible series. Discover Colossians, © 1989, 2000, CRC Publications, 2850 Kalamazoo Ave. SE, Grand Rapids, MI 49560. All rights reserved. Printed in the United States of America on recycled paper. ♻

We welcome your comments. Call us at 1-800-333-8300 or e-mail us at editors@crcpublications.org.

ISBN 1-56212-550-8

10 9 8 7 6 5 4 3

Contents

How to Study 4

Introduction... 5

Glossary of Terms.. 6

Lesson 1
    Grace and Peace 8

Lesson 2
    Jesus Christ: Who He Is and What He Does 10

Lesson 3
    Totally Committed to a Mystery..................................... 13

Lesson 4
    Keep the Focus... 16

Lesson 5
    Putting on New Clothes 19

Lesson 6
    Living with Each Other... 22

Lesson 7
    Christ in You, the Hope of Glory 25

Evaluation Questionnaire

How to Study

The questions in this study booklet will help you discover for yourself what the Bible says. This is inductive Bible study—no one will tell you what the Bible says or what to believe. You will discover the message for yourself. Questions are the key to inductive Bible study. Through questions you will search for the writers' thoughts and ideas. The prepared questions in this booklet are designed to help you in your quest for answers. You can and should ask your own questions too. The Bible comes alive with meaning for many people as they discover for themselves the exciting truths it contains. Our hope and prayer is that this booklet will help the Bible come alive for you.

The questions in this study are designed to be used with the New International Version of the Bible, but other translations can also be used.

Step 1. Read the Bible passage several times. Allow the thoughts and ideas to sink in. Think about its meaning. Ask questions of your own about the passage.

Step 2. Answer the questions, drawing your answers from the passage. Remember that the purpose of the study is to discover what the Bible says. Write your answers in your own words. If you use Bible study aids such as commentaries or Bible handbooks, do so only after completing your own personal study.

Step 3. Apply the Bible's message to your own life and world. Ask yourself these questions: What is this passage saying to me? How does it challenge me? Comfort me? Encourage me? Is there a promise I should claim? A warning I should heed? For what can I give thanks? If you sense God speaking to you in some way, respond in a personal prayer.

Step 4. Share your thoughts with someone else if possible. This will be easiest if you are part of a Bible study group that meets regularly to share discoveries and discuss questions. If you would like to learn of a study group in your area or if you would like more information on how to start a small group Bible study, write to Discover Your Bible, 2850 Kalamazoo Ave. SE, Grand Rapids, MI 49560 or to P.O. Box 5070, STN LCD 1, Burlington, ON L7R 3Y8.

Introduction

Epaphras breathed a sigh of relief. He had made it safely from Colosse to Rome—a dangerous journey in those days. Soon he would see the apostle Paul, who was living in Rome under house arrest. As Epaphras made his way through the streets of Rome to the house where Paul was staying, he thought back to the day he first heard the gospel from Paul himself.

How Paul could set people's hearts on fire with the story of the gospel! Of course, it hadn't been the power of a mere man but the Spirit of God that stirred people's hearts. That same Spirit had enabled Epaphras to take the gospel message back to Colosse and gather a small band of believers into a church. How Epaphras longed to see his little church again! As he hurried over the cobbled streets of Rome, Epaphras said a prayer for that small group of Christians who were holding fast to the truth of the gospel during his absence. He hoped the troublesome false teachers weren't harassing the church while he was gone.

Ah yes, those false teachers . . . the reason for Epaphras's journey to Rome. Who would have thought such empty philosophy could so easily undermine the believers' faith? How could his people listen to such things? "You must live by rules and ceremonies," proclaimed the false teachers. "Only certain food and drink are permissible. You must observe particular traditions and religious festivals—otherwise you are not true believers in Jesus Christ."

The gospel message, once so clear, was now becoming muddied by the brand of religion these false teachers were spreading in the church. God's people in Colosse needed to get back on track. And the great missionary apostle, Paul himself, was just the person to help them do it. Epaphras had faith. He believed that Paul could advise him. Perhaps Paul might even write a letter that Epaphras could take back with him to read to the believers. They would listen to Paul, whose reputation had spread throughout the church from Jerusalem to Rome.

If only Paul would describe for the Colossians the true Christ—the image of God, the Creator; the head of the church; the only One who was ever fully God and fully human. Then the church might be able to see the emptiness of human philosophies and the fullness of Christ their Savior. Epaphras was filled with anticipation. His feet moved more quickly over the dusty streets. Yes, he would ask Paul to send a letter to his little church.

Glossary of Terms

baptism—immersing a person in water (or sprinkling water on a person's head). Going underwater symbolizes a believer's dying to the old way of life (disobedience to God). Coming out of the water symbolizes being raised with Christ to a new way of life (one of obedience to and love for God). Baptism visibly illustrates the fact that God spiritually "washes away" a believer's sin and guilt.

Christ Jesus (or Jesus Christ)—the sinless Son of God, who gave his life as a payment for sin. Christ means "Anointed One" and Jesus means "Savior."

circumcision—the act of cutting away the foreskin of the penis. For the Jews, this ritual symbolized cutting away sin from one's life. The circumcision that God desires, however, is circumcision of the heart—removing sin and evil from one's life and thoughts.

Deity—God.

dominion of darkness—the realm where Satan and evil rule.

Gentiles—people who are not members of the Jewish race.

grace—God's kindness, undeserved favor, and forgiving love, won for believers through Christ's death in their place. Can be explained as God's Riches At Christ's Expense.

gospel—comes from the Greek word meaning "good news." The gospel is the good news that God's Son, Jesus Christ, took the punishment for our sins by dying on the cross. He rose from death and ascended into heaven, where he rules over all things. He will someday return to set up his kingdom in a new heaven and new earth.

holy—pure; set apart to bring glory to God.

inheritance of the saints—eternal life in glory with Christ, a gift of God to all who believe in Jesus as their Savior.

idolatry—worshiping something other than God. It can mean bowing down to a physical image of a god, but Paul uses it in Colossians to mean allowing one's own desires to become more important than God.

new self—the new nature that comes into being when we are cleansed and restored in our relationship with God. Through God's Spirit the believer receives the power to live a new and holy life.

old self—the part of our human nature that still lives in disobedience to God's commands; characterized by anger, malice, greed, selfishness, and immorality.

redemption—the act of buying something back with a ransom payment. Christ "bought back" the lives of all those who believe in him. His death on the cross was payment for the guilt of sin and disobedience that all people carry.

saints—from the Greek word meaning "separated unto God." In the New Testament, it refers to all who live by faith in Jesus Christ.

sensual indulgence—giving in to the desire for physical pleasures.

Spirit—the third person of the Trinity, equal to and one with God the Father and God the Son. The Holy Spirit makes people aware of their sin, brings true faith into their hearts, enables them to live in obedience to God, comforts them, ensures that they will receive all of God's promises, unites them into one community of love, and lives in them forever.

written code—the law of God given in the Old Testament. This code was filled with rules and regulations by which God's people were required to live. Because no one could keep God's law perfectly, the law was a constant reminder of human sin and disobedience. But Christ, by his death, canceled the law's power to accuse and condemn believers.

Lesson 1
Colossians 1:1-14
Grace and Peace

1. ***Colossians 1:1-2***
   a. How does Paul introduce himself? Why might he describe himself this way?

   b. How does Paul describe the Colossian believers?

2. ***Colossians 1:3-8***
   a. What can we learn about the Colossian believers from this passage? What is Paul thankful for?

   b. What does Paul say here about the gospel?

3. ***Colossians 1:9-10a***
   a. According to verse 9, what is Paul's prayer?

   b. If God granted Paul's requests, how would this be evident in the lives of the Colossians?

4. *Colossians 1:10b-12*
   a. What characterizes a life pleasing to the Lord?

   b. What does being strengthened by God's power enable the believer to do?

5. *Colossians 1:13-14*
   a. According to these verses, what has God done for believers?

   b. What do they receive as a result?

6. *Colossians 1:1-14*
   a. How would you define the grace and peace Paul speaks of in verse 2?

   b. What is your impression of the Colossian church?

   c. How do you think the Colossians felt after reading this introduction to Paul's letter?

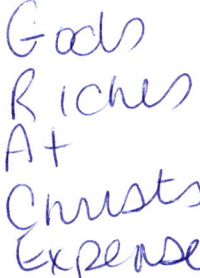

Gods
Riches
At
Christs
Expense

Lesson 2
Colossians 1:15-23

Jesus Christ: Who He Is and What He Does

1. **Colossians 1:15-17**
   The "he" in these verses is Jesus Christ.
   a. What two titles does Paul use for Christ?

   b. What does Paul include in his list of created things?

   c. What is Christ's relationship to the creation?

2. **Colossians 1:18**
   a. What is Christ's relationship to the church?

   b. How did this relationship come about? For what purpose?

3. **Colossians 1:19-20**
   a. What does this passage tell us about Christ?

b. What was God's purpose in sending him?

4. **Colossians 1:21-22**

   a. Contrast the Colossians' former relationship with God to the relationship evident in verse 22.

   b. What brought about the change?

5. **Colossians 1:23**

   a. What was necessary in order for the Colossians to be presented as holy before God?

   b. What does Paul say about the gospel? Why do you think he says these things?

   c. What does Paul say about himself?

6. *Colossians 1:15-23*
   a. Summarize what this passage tells us about Christ. What do you think is the main point Paul wants to get across concerning Christ?

   b. How do you see Paul's plan and purpose for this letter developing?

Lesson 3
Colossians 1:24-2:7
Totally Committed to a Mystery

1. *Colossians 1:24*
    a. What was Paul's attitude toward his suffering? (See also 2 Corinthians 11:24-27.)

    b. How was Paul's suffering related to Christ's afflictions?

    c. For whose sake was Paul suffering?

2. *Colossians 1:25-26*
    a. How does Paul view his position within the church?

    b. What does Paul say about the Word of God?

3. *Colossians 1:27*
    a. According to Paul, what did God choose to do?

b. What is God's mystery? (Try to put it into your own words.)

c. According to verses 26 and 27, to whom has this mystery been made known?

4. **Colossians 1:28-29**
   a. According to these verses, what is Paul's task?

   b. What is his goal?

   c. What does verse 29 imply about Paul's work? How is he able to carry it out?

5. **Colossians 2:1-5**
   a. How does Paul describe his relationship to the Colossians (and to other churches) in verses 1 and 5? What does this tell you about Paul?

   b. In your own words, what does Paul want for the churches?

    c.   What is Paul's purpose for telling the Colossians these things?

6. *Colossians 2:6-7*
    a. How does Paul want the Colossians to live?

    b. Why are they to live this way?

7. *Colossians 1:24-2:7*
    a. On the basis of this passage, how would you write Paul's job description?

    b. According to these verses, what is Paul's attitude toward his work? Toward the churches?

    c. Sum up what these verses tell us about "the mystery that has been kept hidden for ages."

Lesson 4
Colossians 2:8-23
Keep the Focus

Romans 14 1-4

1. *Colossians 2:8*
   a. Against whom or what is Paul warning the Colossians?

   b. How does Paul describe the philosophy being taught in Colosse?

2. *Colossians 2:9-10*
   a. What, in your own words, does Paul say about Christ? ("The Deity" refers to God.)

   b. What did Christ do for the Colossian believers?

3. *Colossians 2:11-12*
   a. What is the difference between human circumcision and circumcision done "by Christ"?

   b. According to Paul, what is the meaning of baptism?

4. **Colossians 2:13-15**
   a. According to verse 13, what was the condition of the Colossian believers before God stepped in?

   b. What did God do for them?

   c. What did Christ's death on the cross accomplish, according to Paul?

5. **Colossians 2:16-17**
   What does Paul say in these verses about food, festivals, celebrations, and observances?

6. **Colossians 2:18-19**
   a. Describe the kind of person Paul warns against in these verses.

   b. If Christ is the "Head" (v. 19), what does "the whole body" refer to? What is Paul saying in this verse?

7. **Colossians 2:20-23**
   a. What warning does Paul give in these verses?

b. What arguments does he use to convince his readers?

8. **Colossians 2:8-23**
   a. What have you learned from this passage about the problems facing the Colossian church?

   b. Summarize in a sentence or two Paul's advice for dealing with these problems.

   c. What can today's church learn from Paul's words in this passage?

Lesson 5
Colossians 3:1-17

Putting on New Clothes

1. *Colossians 3:1-4*

    a. What does Paul want the Colossians to do?

    b. Why are they to do this?

    c. What hope for the future does Paul remind them of?

2. *Colossians 3:5-10*

    a. What were the Colossians to "put to death" and rid themselves of?

    b. Why were they to do this?

    c. What is the difference between the old self and the new self?

3. *Colossians 3:11*
   What does Paul say in this verse about those who are in Christ?

4. *Colossians 3:12-14*
   a. What does Paul ask of his readers in these verses?

   b. Why does he want them to do this?

   c. What is the place of love among all these virtues?

5. *Colossians 3:15-17*
   a. What does Paul ask of his readers in these verses?

   b. How might his suggestions be carried out in everyday life?

   c. What is the motivation for this kind of living?

6. *Colossians 3:1-17*

   a. How would you summarize, in a sentence, what Paul wants the Colossians to do?

   b. According to Paul, what is the motivation for this behavior?

   c. How should Christ's presence in believers' lives affect their attitudes toward their past? Their present? Their future?

Lesson 6
Colossians 3:18-4:18
Living with Each Other

1. *Colossians 3:18-21*
   a. What does Paul ask of Christian family members?

   b. What reasons does he give for this kind of conduct?

2. *Colossians 3:22-4:1*
   a. How does Paul want slaves and masters to behave?

   b. What attitudes and beliefs should motivate them to behave this way?

   c. How would verse 25 serve as both a comfort and a warning to slaves? To masters?

3. *Colossians 4:2-4*
   a. How were the Colossians to pray?

    b.   What is Paul's prayer request for himself (and for Timothy; see 1:1)?

    c.   What does this request reveal about Paul and his goals?

4. **Colossians 4:5-6**

    a.   How does Paul want his readers to behave toward those outside the church?

    b.   Why do you think he wants them to behave this way?

5. **Colossians 4:7-14**

    a.   What do these verses tell you about Paul and his situation? What do they reveal about the people mentioned?

    b.   Epaphras (mentioned in Colossians 1:7-8) was probably the pastor of the Colossian church. What do these verses reveal about his work and character?

6. **Colossians 4:15-18**

    a.   What do these verses tell you about the relationship between the churches in Colosse and Laodicea?

b. What thoughts and feelings are revealed by each of Paul's closing statements in verse 18?

7. *Colossians 3:18-4:18 and review*

   a. According to this letter, what should motivate believers' actions toward others?

   b. How would you sum up Paul's message to the Colossians in a sentence or two? What do you think is his most important point?

   c. What is most meaningful to you?

Lesson 7
Selected verses from Colossians
Christ in You, the Hope of Glory

1. *Colossians 1:21*
    a. What is the nature of people's relationship with God, apart from Christ?

    b. According to this verse, what is the cause of the problem?

2. *Colossians 3:5-9a*
    a. Describe the former lifestyle of the unsaved Colossians.

    b. What would be the result of continuing in this lifestyle?

3. *Colossians 1:19-20, 22*
    a. What did God want to accomplish by sending Jesus?

    b. What was the means by which this goal was accomplished?

   c.   How does God view those who are reconciled to him?

4. **Colossians 2:13-15**
   a. Why does Paul call the unsaved Colossians "dead"?

   b. How did they come to life?

   c. What should now be their view of the written code (or Old Testament laws)? Of the powers and authorities (Satan and his angels)?

5. **Colossians 3:1-4**
   a. How should the Colossians' lifestyle differ from the way they lived when they were spiritually dead?

   b. How would their newfound faith provide motivation for a different lifestyle?

6. **Colossians 1:9-14**
   a. What has God done for believers? What does God do for them continually?

    b.   What are they motivated to do in return?

7. *Colossians 3:15-17*
    a. What is to be the ruling principle in the life of believers?

    b. How does this ruling principle affect individuals in their daily lives? How does it affect the church?

    c. How would you describe, in one sentence, the spirit in which believers are to think, speak, and act?

8. *Summary*
    a. Based on your study of Colossians, how would you describe the condition of people without God?

    b. How does this condition change when a person is made alive with Christ?

    c. How does being raised with Christ affect a person's thoughts, actions, and words?

Wrap-Up

Listen now to what God is saying to you.

You may be aware of things in your life that keep you from coming near to God. You may envision God as unsympathetic, angry, or punishing. You may feel that you don't know how to pray or come near to God.

Listen to what God is saying to you through the saving love of Christ Jesus. God is an understanding, loving Father who longs to come near to you, lift you up, and give you the gift of grace. Christ knows firsthand what it's like to live in a sinful, broken world. He has already taken the punishment for your sin, clearing the way for you to come near to him.

Coming near to God is not always easy, but it is simple—as simple as A-B-C:

—**A**dmit that you have sinned and that you need God's forgiveness.
—**B**elieve that God loves you and that Jesus has already paid the price for your sins.
—**C**ommit your life to God in prayer, asking God to forgive your sins, make you his child, and fill you with the Holy Spirit.

Prayer of Commitment

Here is a prayer of commitment to Jesus Christ. If you long to be in a loving relationship with him, pray this prayer. If you have already made that commitment to Jesus, use this prayer for renewal and praise.

"Dear God, I come to you simply and honestly to confess that I have sinned and that sin is a part of who I am. And yet I know that you listen to sinners who are truthful before you. So I come with empty hands and heart, asking for forgiveness.

"I confess that only through faith in Jesus Christ can I come to you. I confess my need for a Savior, and I thank you, Jesus Christ, for dying on the cross to pay the price for my sins. I ask that you forgive my sins and count me among those who are righteous in your sight. Remove the guilt that accompanies sin and bring me to my heavenly Father.

"Give me your Holy Spirit now to help me pray and to teach me from your Word. Be my faithful God and help me to faithfully serve you. It is only because of the atoning sacrifice of Jesus Christ that I come to you, loving God. In Jesus' name I pray. Amen."

Evaluation Questionnaire

DISCOVER COLOSSIANS

As you complete this study, please fill out this questionnaire to help us evaluate the effectiveness of our materials. Please be candid. Thank you.

1. Was this a home group ___ or a church-based ___ program? What church?

2. Was the study used for
   ___ a community evangelism group?
   ___ a community grow group?
   ___ a church Bible study group?

3. How would you rate the materials?

   Study Guide
   ___ excellent ___ very good ___ good ___ fair ___ poor

   Leader Guide
   ___ excellent ___ very good ___ good ___ fair ___ poor

4. What were the strengths?

5. What were the weaknesses?

6. What would you suggest to improve the material?

7. In general, what was the experience of your group?

Your name (optional) _____

Address _____

8. Other comments:

(Please fold, tape, stamp, and mail. Thank you.)

CRC Publications
2850 Kalamazoo Ave. SE
Grand Rapids, MI 49560-0300